sally

Meira ~ Have fun with Sally's silly stories.

Life With Sally

Still Spinnin' Tails

by

Tricia L. McDonald

Splattered Ink Press
Michigan

Life With Sally
Still Spinnin' Tails

By Tricia L. McDonald

First Printing: December 2011

ISBN – 978-0-9848542-0-2

Published by:

Splattered Ink Press
16637 Rich Street
Grand Haven, MI 49417
splatteredinkpress.com

Printed in the United States of America

Dedicated to my muse ... Sally, the little white dog.

Acknowledgments

My very first thank you is to all of the wonderful Sally fans. Thank you for loving this little dog.

Thank you to my son, Jacob, who, once again, produced an amazing cover. His talent continues to astound me. To my daughter, Nicole, who still shakes her head over my continuous Sally saga, but does so with love.

To my husband, Mike, who has never complained about often being fodder for the stories. Okay, maybe once or twice he has winced.

Thank you to my wonderful friend, Ellen Hosafros, who is always encouraging and ready to edit at a moment's notice.

To my writing groups and friends who workshop my Sally stories over and over and over with me.

And again, to everyone who has taken the time to tell me how much they love to read the Sally stories, either in person or by e-mail, thank you.

I am on a fantastic Sally journey and enjoying every minute.

Table of Contents

She's Not the Boss of Me!

I flop into the recliner, pull the fleece blanket up to my chin and kick up the foot rest. Aaah! Nice breather at the end of a cold, busy day. But I have a writing assignment due tomorrow, so I can't totally zone out on TV or a book. I drag my computer to my lap and turn it on.

Staring at the screen, I hear Sally's toenails click over the hardwood floor toward me. She stops beside the chair and looks up.

"Not right now, Sally," I say without looking at her. I know what she wants. My lap. And sometimes she can work me with that little cute face of hers. But not right now.

My fingers fly across the keyboard as I transcribe a handwritten story from my Seniors Writing Group. Typing comes easy to me since I have been doing it in some form for over 30 years. Wow! Thirty years? I'm feeling old.

I turn a page and continue transferring the words. As I glance back at the notes, I catch a glimpse of Miss Sally, who is standing in the exact same spot next to the chair. Her gaze is still directed at me, nothing else, just me.

"Sally, I said not now."

My head swivels from the paper to the screen, back to the paper, back to the screen. Sally walks to the end of the chair and nudges the bottom of my feet with her long nose.

"What is she doing?" Mike asks.

"Trying to convince me to let her up on my lap."

"Poor Sally."

"Go get on your dad's lap," I tell her.

"Come here, Sal." Mike pats his lap.

Sally wags her tail, but continues staring at me. She makes one of her pterodactyl noises. I can't really describe it, other than it sounds really, really odd.

"Can't you just squeeze her up there?"

"Not while I'm typing." I continue looking from the paper to the screen and type faster so the princess doesn't have to suffer any longer than necessary. What this really means is she'll get her way sooner, rather than later.

Mike walks into the kitchen and opens the refrigerator door. To Sally, this sound doesn't mean refrigerator, it means cheese or chicken or lunchmeat. And food wins over mom's lap anytime.

I use the distraction to slow my typing, thus reducing the errors that I have to keep going back to correct. I'm in a nice rhythm when I hear the tell-tale click click click again. Then I feel the nose nudging, followed by the odd little noises.

"Sally, hold on I'm almost done."

I sneak a glance as she lays her little chin on the foot rest. She looks up at me, her black eyes filled with lap long-ing.

"How can you ignore that cute face?" Mike says.

"I have to finish this, that's how." I look over at him. "Plus, she's the dog and I'm the owner. I make the decisions. She's not the boss of me."

Mike spits up Diet Coke through his laughter.

"What?" I say.

"Oh yeah, no confusion about who's the boss in that relationship."

I sneer at him, and then go back to my typing. Sally's chin is still resting next to my foot. Her eyes remain focused on my face.

Socks, our cat, goes into a frenzy with the catnip toy. He runs through the room, batting it from side to side. There is a slight wagging from Sally's tail, but that's all.

The phone rings and Mike gets up to answer it. Sally lifts her head and glances his way, then returns it to its resting position. The stare-down continues.

This is ridiculous! She is right in my sight line with the computer screen, so every time I look at it, I look at her.

Mike walks back in the room and sits down. "Just let her up there for a few minutes."

When I look down at her, Sally stands with her front paws on the foot rest. She smiles at me with that huge grin and her tail is wagging non-stop. Socks runs by again and gets whapped in the face with the little white tail.

Sighing, I put the computer on the table next to my chair and Sally doesn't even wait for me to help her onto my lap. She is crawling up before I settle back in the chair. She sits and gives me a couple of ear nibbles, then curls, tucks her nose and starts snoring.

"She can only stay up here for a few minutes," I say to Mike as I rub Sally's ears.

"Yeah right, boss."

HO HO Sally

Sally backs into my legs.

"It's okay, Sal," I say. I nudge her forward and close the door behind me.

We're visiting the Must Love Dogs Boutique and Spa in Grand Haven for the big event ... Santa is here!

The door opens behind me and I scoop Sally into my arms and step aside as more dogs and their owners arrive. The place is full to the brim with dogs of every size and shape. It is a fur fest.

"I wonder if that's Sally?" a woman says, pointing at the squirming dog in my arms. She tells the woman next to her about a column in <u>Cats and Dogs Magazine</u> where a woman writes about a miniature bull terrier named Sally.

"Yes, this is Sally," I say. I hold her muscled, trembling body close.

"Oh my gosh," the woman says. "I can't believe I get to meet Sally in person."

A ripple goes through the store and I hear "Sally" repeated by several people. Heads turn to stare.

"She's a little nervous," I explain to the woman petting her. Sally is shaking in my arms. She burrows her long snout into my armpit.

"She wouldn't be nervous if she had her rake," the woman says. I had written about Sally's obsession with the lawn rake in one of my columns. I laugh and imagine Sally dragging her rake around this room. There would be bruises on all the shins, both human and canine.

I get in line and pay for Sally's photo with Santa. The money will go to Pet Pantry, a non-profit program that assists low-income families with their pets. I know there's little hope of getting a good photo due to Sally's camera-phobia, but I pay for two photos anyway, doubling my chances.

I spot a holiday collar in red and green decked out with tiny bells. How adorable! And since my husband, Mike, is not here to tell me it is too cutesy, I put one on Sally.

She shakes her head and the bells tinkle. In my arms she rears her head back, trying to get away from the sound, and smacks me in the mouth with her brick-like head. *That's gonna leave a mark*, I think as I run my tongue over my already swelling lip.

I set Sally down and we walk around the room, meeting the other dogs and owners. The truth is, I walk around the room and Sally trots around my feet, tangling me with her leash. Sitting down is the only way I won't trip and fall on my face.

I find floor space in a semi-secluded spot against a wall of shelves and sit down. Sally dives into my lap.

HO HO Sally

The door to the back room (Santa's photo shop) opens, and seven greyhounds spill out. Seven greyhounds! I jump to my feet to avoid getting trampled. Now the room is wall-to-wall dogs and people. Jodi, a Pet Pantry volunteer, walks by and stops when she sees me.

"Hey, Sally's here!" she shouts over the din of conversation and barking. This starts another buzz of "Sally" throughout the store. I'm beaming; Sally is still trembling.

The herd of greyhounds leave, and more dogs arrive. Jodi calls Sally's name and we follow her to Santa's room.

"I told them all about Sally," she says. Inside we find 'them,' Santa on a comfy loveseat and his photo elf assistant, camera in hand.

I set Sally in Santa's lap. She is having none of this. No way, no how, and where is the door? She tries to jump off, but Santa hangs on. His grip slips and she is back on the floor and trying to escape.

I scoop her up and sit down next to Santa. I try a sneak-move by setting her on my lap, then easing her over to his lap. She assures me she is not that naive. I'm sweating and blowing hair out of my face as I try to hold her on his lap. The elf is snapping photos. Oh no! I don't want to be in the picture--just Sally. By now, she is off Santa's lap again.

We decide a time-out is a good idea and Jodi offers Sally a treat. But she's searching for an escape and has no interest in the snack. Sally turning down food? This is serious.

I pick her up, nuzzle her nose and whisper sweet little nothings in her pointed pink ear. She calms and I put her back

7

in Santa's lap. Her paws get tangled in his beard, the elf snaps a few more photos and we call it quits. We're all exhausted.

In the car, I replace Sally's holly-jolly collar with her purple harness. She is panting.

She gives me the eye on the drive home and guilt washes over me for putting her through such an ordeal just for a photo.

So I stop and buy us popcorn, which makes the rest of the drive a happy munchfest.

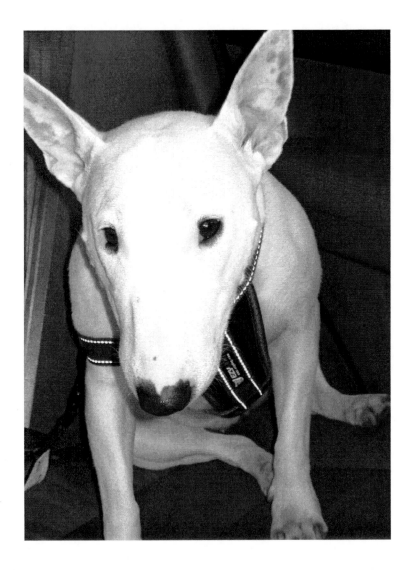

Photo Shoot Disaster

Self-publishing a book involves wearing a lot of different hats. But when it comes to the cover of the book, I turn to my son, Jake. He is, after all, Sally's personal photographer.

I suggest we use a photo that has already been taken for the cover of <u>Life With Sally: Little White Dog Tails</u>.

"No way, mom," is Jake's response.

"How about a drawing for the cover?" I say.

"No."

"How about just words?"

"No. You write the book and let me handle the cover, okay?"

I loosen the grip on my need to control and trust in his expertise. Wise move.

Jake is a film and video major at Grand Valley State University in Michigan and as such, he has access to a room and photo equipment. All I have to do is show up with the princess.

On the night of the camera shoot, I walk Sally around the campus, waiting for Jake to get out of his class. Sally bounds along the walkways, sniffing at bushes, trees and pant legs.

A duck quacks and my eyes search a nearby pond. No ducks. We continue up the walkway, and I hear the duck again. I look around for the little quacker and realize the quacking is coming from my pocket. The ringtone I have for Jake is a duck. I punch the speak button.

"Hello?"

"What are you doing?" Jake says.

"What are you talking about?" I say.

"Mom, I'm right behind you. Turn around."

Jake is six feet, seven inches tall with a scruffy red beard and a smile that radiates. He's striding up the sidewalk behind us. Sally sees him and pulls at her leash. I let go and she tears toward him, leaping at his legs.

"Seriously, why weren't you answering your phone?" he asks when he reaches me.

"I thought it was a real duck."

He grins and shakes his head. "I wonder about you sometimes."

In the reserved room, I let Sally acclimate herself to the smells and sounds. I hope this will make her more relaxed and the photo shoot will be a piece of cake. If only I weren't so naive.

Jake sets up the lights, camera and back drop, and then shoots a couple of author photos of me. Our plan is to take Sally's photos last so she'll be tired and easier to work with. I never learn.

Once we're done with my photos, Jake rearranges the lights. I sit on the black velvet backdrop and Sally wanders around me, her long white nose sniffing like an aardvark on an ant trail. It's peaceful and I'm lulled into a sense of tranquility, until a pole crashes down and smacks me on the head.

"Mom, are you okay?"

I touch my hand to the lump forming on my head. No blood. That's good. I run a finger over my nose. A bump, but it doesn't feel broken. Again, good.

"Mom, please say something."

"What happened?" I ask. What a shock, the pole crashing is Sally-related. She had bumped into a camera stand, which scared her. She leapt backward, crashing into another stand that knocked over the pole, which landed on my head. Nothing is easy with this little dog.

Now she's crouching under a chair, her white nose sticking out from under the seat. So much for an easy photo shoot. I wrestle her out. I give her lots of baby talk and snuggles while Jake sets everything up again.

I set Sally on the backdrop, holding her in place while Jake adjusts the camera.

"Sally," he says. She looks up at him, I let go and roll out of the picture frame. Her gaze follows me.

"Sally," Jake says again and snaps his fingers. She jumps to her feet and walks toward me.

"No, no, Sal." I put her back in the spot. I let go, and she slumps. I prop her back up.

"Mom, your legs are in the photo."

I straddle her, my legs spread as far as I can without compromising my pants. She walks away. I give her a treat and lead her back.

"See if you can get her to look up."

I straddle her and hold a treat over her head. She looks up. All the way up. I lower the treat, she lowers her head. Great photo, except for the human arm hanging over her.

This goes on for months. Okay, it feels like months. By the end of the session, Jake has taken at least 100 photos, but he's still not sure we have a good one.

"I can't do this anymore," I say.

"Me, either."

We pack up and leave.

As I walk in the house later, my husband says, "How did it go?"

"Don't ask," I say as I rub the bump on my nose.

Sally heads straight to her pillow. I reach into the freezer for ice.

Photo Shoot Disaster

Family Dynamics

Before there was Sally, there was Harry, a 20-pound border terrier with an 80-pound attitude. Everyone knew Harry was the alpha—not only in the house, but in the neighborhood. Harry was with us only nine years when he was diagnosed with an inoperable tumor. Within three months, he was gone.

The following day, Mary, our lab/cocker mix, walked to the end of the driveway and laid down. Every day she would lay there for hours, her head on her paws, waiting for Harry to come back. The spark in her eyes disappeared and her shiny red coat started to dull. Mary was in mourning.

Cue the little white dog.

Curled in a ball on her pillow in the living room, Mary was not ready for the newest family member, a little piglet-looking puppy. As soon as I put her on the floor, Sally bounded right over to Mary. No fear. Until Mary leapt to her feet and gave a sneer. Her reaction to her new playmate was not happiness . It was more like "what is this?" and "get it out of here." She tried to do some investigative sniffing, which proved impossible due to the spinning the pig-like creature was doing. And within minutes, Mary was watching from the couch, a place Sally could not yet reach.

Five years later, Mary has no hiding places, no safe spots where she can get away from Sally. Yet Sally knows when to leave Mary alone, which is most of the time. At 11 years old, Mary is going deaf and her cataracts are getting worse. Her increasingly white face shows her age.

There was a time when Mary would egg Sally into a chase, and then sprint away from her as if Sally was standing still. Now Mary only chases her ball and tires out long before the ball thrower. When she's had enough, she collects her ball and lies down. It doesn't matter if she's in snow or grass, when she's done, she's done.

Sally seems to know this. She used to grab Mary's ball and tease her with it, trying to get her to chase her. Now, when the matriarch lies down, Sally leaves her alone. For the most part, anyway.

So who gets the Sally-harassment now? Our cats. Socks and Stan are 12-year-old litter mates. They have never been apart, yet they have very different personalities. Black-and-white Stan disappears when people visit. After they leave, he comes out of his hiding spot. Gray-and-white Socks never disappears.

As a puppy, Sally was smaller than Socks and Stan. This gave the cats an advantage, and Socks used it. He would sit on the edge of the couch or the coffee table, and when Sally walked by, he'd swat her. Sally would scoot forward, then turn around and run back and forth in front of Socks, yapping. Socks would watch her, yawn, curl into a ball and take a nap. Sally would sit and stare.

Sally is now bigger than both cats. And you know what they say about paybacks.

Sally's favorite game with Socks is to corner him and then dart back and forth, not letting him get away. At first, Socks gives Sally his "you're nuts" look. Then he bats at her long white snout, but Sally's head is rock-like and his paws bounce off. I don't think she even feels his slaps.

At some point, Sally charges and pins Socks. And Socks starts meowing like something is killing him.

"Sally, leave Socks alone," I say.

Sally leaps back and Socks stands, regaining his composure. I leave the room. Within seconds I hear Socks meowing again, and sure enough, Sally has him pinned. I scold Sally and she walks to her kennel with her head hanging. She knows how to work the pitiful look.

One time I left the room, but peeked around the doorway and watched. Socks walked over to Sally, rubbed his head under her chin, and then swatted her in the chops. Sally crouched and pounced, pinning Socks to the floor. The meowing started. But this time I left them alone with their game.

The other day I heard a ruckus outside the bathroom door. There was a cat on either side of Sally. One swatted at Sally's nose, and when she turned toward the offender, the other one lunged for her tail. Sally spun around to head-butt the tail grabber and got smacked in the nose by a paw. A kitty tag-team!

I had hoped for some furry snuggling in our household, but Sally and Mary don't curl together and nap. And the dogs don't sleep with the cats. But neither is there any spitting or snarling.

So it's all good.

Bathroom Etiquette

"That's just wrong," my son says. He walks into the living room with Sally close at his heels.

"What's just wrong?" I say.

"Sally kept trying to get on my lap."

"How is that wrong?"

"I was sitting on the toilet."

"Oh, my fault."

When I became a mother, I no longer had privacy in the bathroom. My first realization of this was when I had to take my infant daughter into the bathroom just so I could take a shower. She sat in her baby carrier, and I peeked around the shower curtain as much as possible to remind her that yes, I was still there. Later, as my children became toddlers, I found it was safer to take them into the bathroom with me than leave them alone. A creative toddler can wreak havoc in the time it takes to pee.

So began a lifetime of bathroom sharing. As the kids got older I shut the door, but didn't lock it because I never knew when I was going to have to make a fast exit. A fight between siblings in the next room, or a blood curdling scream required a referee or a spider-eliminator.

Now that both of my children have moved out, it's too late to change this habit. I never latch the bathroom door. And an unlatched door to a little white dog means she is coming in.

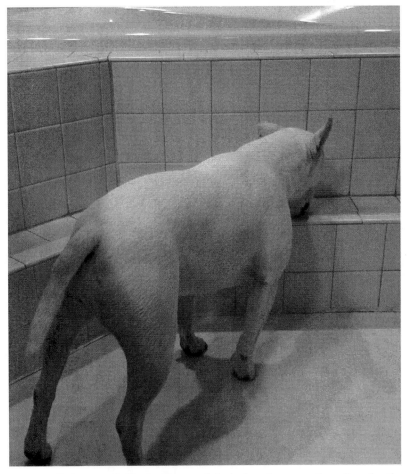

Princess Sally believes this is her house, thus her bathroom. And if the door is shut, she pushes it open. Boundaries mean nothing to her.

Whenever I go into the bathroom, she follows and sits on the rug in front of me. As I settle onto the throne, she starts spinning and chasing her tail. Who needs a book or a magazine when you have a spinning dog to entertain you? It's comical to watch until her rockish head slams into my shins. Then, not so funny.

"Ouch, Sally!" I rub the bruise forming on my leg. She sits on her haunches and hangs her head. She looks up at me. Her head doesn't move, only her eyes. It's funny. I laugh. The happy spinning begins again. Occasionally I bring a novel to the bathroom, and as soon as I open it Sally puts her paws on my knees and nudges the book away. Is that normal? Or crazy?

And don't get me started on the shower. She doesn't get in the shower with me, of course. That would be ridiculous. However, she sits outside the shower door and waits. When I step out, Sally starts licking my legs. Creepy? Sounds like it, doesn't it? But it isn't creepy at all. In fact, it is, shall I say, tender? soothing? helpful? A great way to avoid bending over to dry below my knees? Okay, it's a little creepy.

If I get into the bathtub, Sally will lean against the edge. But only if there is no splashing. Even if a little splashing occurs, she is out of there.

Then the cats wander in, perch on the edge of the bathtub and stare at the bubbles. There has been more than one occasion where Stan or Socks has batted at a bubble and slipped into the tub. Their paws barely touch the bottom before they fly out of the water, through the bathroom and onto the bed where they dry themselves. A cat falling into the water causes splashing, so Sally, who's afraid of splashing, does her ninja slide under the bed and stays there.

I question why the water in the bathroom is more delectable than the water in the pet dishes. I'm always fighting with the cats about drinking out of the toilets, or licking the faucets. And once my legs are dry, Sally will lick the floor where I was standing. And all three of them will lap at the water on the edge of the bathtub. Yet there is a fresh bowl of water in the kitchen for them. Go figure.

"I'm going to take a shower," Jake says as he walks out of the room. Sally strolls behind him.

"You might want to shut the door," I say. "And make sure it latches."

I hear the water running and then the sound of a little white nose bumping against the door.

A Sleepover Gone Awry

She's baaaaack! Little Sophie is spending her spring break with us again. Let the games begin!

Day one: Sophie, a black Schnoodle, has become Velcro dog, bumping her petite nose against my legs as she trots behind me. Sally bounces at Sophie, inviting her to play. Sophie is not so inclined. That night, Sally and I head to the guest room to sleep. Mike and I don't sleep together when Sophie visits. The last time we tried, we woke to Sophie growling at Sally. That's not a good sound any time, but especially when it is coming from the pillow beside your head in the middle of the night.

Day two: Sally and I drag ourselves down the stairs. Between the wind blowing the curtains (on a warm April evening) and the creaky overhead fan, Sally didn't sleep well in the guest room. Noises seem to bother her on occasion. Last night was one of those occasions. And that translated into 'I' didn't sleep well. Sophie barks at us as we stumble into the kitchen. Really Sophie?

When Mike and I head out for the day we put Sophie in her kennel. When we get back, she greets us with her ear-splitting yipping. In between Sophie visits, I forget about the fingernails-on-the-blackboard-noise. It is unbelievable it can come from this little cuddly teddy bear of a dog. But it does. Mike and I race each other to the kennel to let her out. After that, we never put her back in there.

I walk around like a zombie due to sleep deprivation, and Mike offers to sleep in the guest room with Sophie the next three nights. Sally and I stretch out on our bed with great abandon.

Day five: Mike leaves for a trip down south with the guys. Uh oh! This is going to present a new sleeping challenge. Sophie and Sally in the same bed.

"Everything will be fine," I say to Mike. "Go have fun."

He leaves. I slump onto the couch and Sophie jumps onto my lap. "This is going to be a nightmare," I say to her. She licks my nose, curls into a ball and falls asleep.

I stay up past my normal bedtime and run the dogs outside several times. I want us all to be exhausted when we hit the bed. When I can barely stand, I rearrange the pillows and crawl into the middle of the bed. Sally is waiting for me in her usual spot on my left side. I pat the bed and call Sophie. She jumps up on my right. Sally does a Batman leap over my body and bumps Sophie with her snout. Sophie falls off the bed. Not boding well for a good night's sleep.

I pat the bed again and Sophie looks at me, cocking her head as if to say "Are you nuts?" Sally's whole body is wiggling with playtime anticipation as she looks down at Sophie.

"Sally, get back over here," I say. I pull her to my left. Then I beg and plead with Sophie to come back up. When she still doesn't move, I plop back onto my pillow. She whines. Sally wriggles. I put my left hand on her to keep her still and pat the bed with my right hand. Sophie jumps up and curls against my right side. Success!

I lay still, wedged in on my right by a little black dog and on my left by a little white one. I can't move without upsetting the whole arrangement. But no one is growling. And when I chance turning my head, I see that Sophie's eyes are closed. When I turn my head back, Sally is giving me the evil eye.

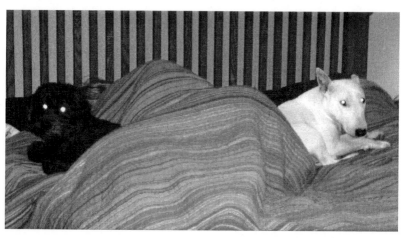

I burrow into the covers and sigh. This might work after all.

Mary, meanwhile, has arranged herself on the pillows on the floor. She is oblivious to Sophie's visit. All is well.

Except, the light is still on. And I forgot to turn on the fan. But if I move, it is going to upset this Zen-like mood. Maybe I can sleep with the light on. I close my eyes and focus on my breathing. Long deep breaths, in and out. Relax.

The stupid light is bugging me.

I lean over Sophie and reach for the bedside table. In my flailing, I hit the lamp and it crashes to the floor. In one incredibly graceful move Sally jumps from the bed and dives into her kennel. Mary skids toward the door. Sophie, trapped underneath me, is yipping. I roll over, she leaps to the floor. This is so not good.

I untangle myself from the blankets, right the lamp, coax Sally out of her kennel and back into bed. After turning on the fan and shutting off the light, I pat the bed. Sophie jumps up and snuggles into my right side; Sally has me pinned on my left. Mary sneaks back to her floor pillows. And this is how we sleep. Me, like a mummy, and the dogs stretched out beside me in perfect harmony!

Until 5:00 a.m. when they all decide it is time for a potty break!

Diving for Pee

"Sally, did you pee on yourself?" Anna, our groomer's assistant, examines Sally's pink belly. "Oh, it looks like she might have a bladder infection," she says. "You might want to have that looked at."

"I'm taking her to the vet tomorrow for her yearly visit, so I'll have them check it out," I say.

"Make sure you take a urine sample with you," Anna says.

And that brief sentence has a lot packed into it.

Over my lifetime I have given urine samples. No big deal. Write your name on the plastic container with the black Sharpie, pee into the cup, and leave it on the shelf in the doctor's bathroom. Oh, and don't forget to wash your hands. The directions, in case you couldn't figure it out on your own, are hanging on the wall.

If there was a need for a urine sample when my children were small, again it was no big deal. Hold the cup under their urine stream. Of course, there was a larger margin for getting peed on with this method, but it worked nonetheless.

But getting a urine sample from a dog, a whole new situation. Harry, our deceased border terrier, had been easy to get a sample from since he was a pee-on-command dog.

As soon as he heard, "Harry, take care of business" he would life his leg and pee. Hold the container under the stream and you're done.

But Sally is timid about new things. Sally won't eat out of a new bowl. Sally won't enter the living room if the furniture has been rearranged. How was I going to make getting a urine sample happen?

My first plan — get my husband, Mike, to do it. While getting ready for bed that night, I tell him we need to get a sample from Sally.

"When you let the dogs out to pee, will you give it a try?" I ask.

He nods his head with enthusiasm. Okay, I am adding the enthusiasm part. In truth, I don't know if he even nodded his head, because I am yelling from the bedroom and he is in the living room.

A few minutes later I hear him open the front door and call the dogs. He runs into the kitchen, rummages through the plastic-ware cupboard, and runs outside. What is going on? I have already forgotten about the pee specimen since I passed the responsibility on to him. Then I remember. I wait with anticipation.

The door opens and Sally bounds in and flies onto my bed. Mike stands at the bedroom door with an empty container.

"No luck?" I say.

He turns it upside down.

"Okay then, guess I'll try in the morning," I say, disappointed.

Sally wakes me at 4:00 a.m. to go out and I pick up the container on our way outside. But in my exhausted state I decide it just isn't the right time to try such a feat.

At 7:00 a.m. it is time. I pull my huge fluffy bathrobe over my pajamas and slip my feet into my sloppy black

boots. As I pass the mirror, I decide I should take the dogs out the back door so as not to frighten the neighbors driving past the front of the house. I open the door and Mary and Sally run across the deck, do a superman leap onto the grass, and run through the gargoyle garden and into the woods. I am running behind them, bathrobe flapping and plastic container held in the air like a scepter.

"Sally, wait," I yell. "Don't pee yet." She turns, looks at me, and squats. I stop, drop my head in defeat and walk back to the house. She catches up with me and grabs the container out of my hand. She runs a few feet, drops to the ground, and starts ripping it apart. I snatch it away from her and decide to try the Harry pee-on-command approach.

"Sally, take care of business," I say. She looks at me, looks at the container and does a happy spin. "Sally, take care of business," I repeat with a stern voice.

She squats and I trip over my bathrobe as I dive to catch a few drops of urine. Sally takes one look at me diving toward her and bolts. This is so not working.

I drag myself into the house and kick off the boots.

"Get anything?" Mike asks.

I turn the container upside down.

After lunch I decide to give it another try. Her appointment is in an hour so I really have to make this work. This time I take her outside alone so she and Mary won't chase each other into the woods.

She walks to a mole hole and jams her nose into it.

"Sally, take care of business."

She jogs to the deck and sniffs along the side where wild bunnies go in and out.

"Come on Sally, take care of business."

She walks under the bird feeder and nibbles at the broken sunflower seeds.

"Sally, please take care of business."

A chickadee flutters above her. Sally ducks. I chuckle.

"Sally, please, please, please take care of business."

She trots to a tree and starts eating the long grass around it.

"Give me a break," I say as I start turning to the door. But out of the corner of my eye I see the beginnings of a squat.

I whip back around and thrust the plastic container under Sally. She jumps but keeps peeing and my hand follows. When she finishes, there is a little yellowish orange liquid in the bowl, and lots more on my hand. Eeeeew!

Now I just have to get a cover on it before the little white dog trips me and I spill it.

Stoic Sally?

I balance the plastic container of Sally pee on my lap while I keep my right hand on Sally's body and steer with my left. I have no idea how I'm keeping the car on the road as we drive to the vet's office. Sally needs a health certificate that will allow her entry into the PetExpo for her paw signing of <u>Life With Sally: Little White Dog Tails</u>.

At the vet's office, Sally jumps out of the car, wiggling with excitement. Everyone is happy to see her and her tail wags like crazy. I hand off the sample and Sally and I wait our turn.

"Okay, Sally," the vet tech says. Sally weighs in at 29 pounds. Up a few pounds from last year, but aren't we all?

In the exam room, the vet asks, "Was Sally peeing around the house?"

"No."

"Was she licking herself a lot?"

"No."

"Did she seem to be in pain when she was urinating?"

"No."

She tells me Sally has a severe bladder infection. She has blood in her urine and crystals have formed. She talks about red blood cells and how there were too many to count, and now I'm wishing I had paid more attention in science class because I don't understand what she is saying. I'm a writer. I know how to put words on a page. Cells, microscopes and the like I don't understand.

"Is it bad?" I ask.

"It's not good."

Guilt settles over me like a wet blanket.

"Would she feel pain from this infection?"

"Yes," the vet says. "But these dogs are pretty stoic."

Now I'm really confused. Sally is a wimp, and she has not acted like she was in pain at all. Not even a little whimper.

The vet listens to Sally's heart and says she has a strong heartbeat. Sally is leaning against me and I wonder if the vet is hearing my racing heartbeat through Sally's body. How could I miss that my little Sally is sick? *I am a bad mom.*

The vet checks Sally's booty, legs, paws and moves to her teeth.

"Uh oh," she says as she peels Sally's lips away from her gums.

I don't want to hear anyone in the medical field say "Uh oh." But maybe it is just a sliver from her favorite toy, the rake.

The vet examines Sal's mouth and says she needs to go to a vet that specializes in animal dentistry. Seems that Sally may have an abscessed tooth and the infection is leaking from the inside out, through a hole in her gum. The vet shows me the black hole and I throw up a little in my mouth.

Guilt is about to explode through the top of my head.

"I'm so sorry, Sal," I burrow my face into her neck. *I am a bad, bad mom.* My little dog is falling apart while I worried about whether we were going to have enough books for her paw signing. And since when did Sally become stoic?

"Has she been eating?" the vet asks.

"Yes, well, no, well she has strange eating habits," I say. "She has been eating, but if the phone rings, she runs away from her dish. Or if the refrigerator door is opened, she won't eat. But her food is always gone."

There is no doubt; I am going to get the award for bad dog mom of the year. When I go home, the Animal Protective Services will be waiting at the door. "We got a report that you are a bad Sally mom," a guy in a green uniform is going to say. Then he is going to reach for Sally.

"Well, her weight is fine," the vet interrupts my misery.

That's right. If she wasn't eating, her weight would be down, not up.

The vet leaves the room to prepare medication and I smother Sally's pointed white nose with kisses.

"I'm sorry, Sal," I say. She pushes her nose toward my pocket holding her treats. I fish one out and she chomps it down. No wincing, no whimpering, and no careful chewing. Maybe she is stoic.

At home, I call Mike.

"Sally is a mess," I say. "She has a bad bladder infection and an abscessed tooth with a hole in her gum where the infection is leaking from the inside out." I wince.

"Well, we know she hasn't been in any pain."

"The vet said she has but these dogs are very stoic."

Mike laughs. "Tricia, she is not stoic."

I'm offended. I can say she is a wimp because I say it with love. "She is stoic," I repeat.

"Wimp."

"Stoic."

"Maybe a little wimpy, but right now she is really sick." I reach for the treat bowl and Sally starts spinning. I hang up the phone and Sally runs to the bedroom. She dives into the pillows on the bed, knocking them onto the floor, then tears from one end to the other.

Sick? Really?

Say Ahh!

I grab the door handle of the veterinary exam room, bolt to my car and call Mike.

"Sally update," he says.

"I just left her with the dental vet." My voice catches.

"Are you okay?" he asks.

That's all it takes. The tears come fast as I choke out a "no."

"I had to leave her there," I cry. "And she watched me walk out of the room and her eyes looked so sad." I feel lightheaded and take a deep breath.

"She's going to be okay."

"I know, but she looked so scared and I just left her." I sniffle.

"What did the vet say about her?"

"They are going to anesthetize her enough to check out her teeth, and then he's going to call me."

"Call me when you hear something."

I drive in a daze to my office and keep busy while waiting for the phone to ring. After what seems like an eternity, but is only an hour, Dr. Moore calls. He's the doggy dental specialist at Harborfront Hospital for Animals.

"Sally has malocclusion degeneration," he says.

"Say what?"

He continues with an explanation that sounds like a medical textbook. Sally's jaw is out of line and that caused the upper and lower canines to rub together. They have probably been like that her whole life, all five years.

Sally doesn't have an abscessed tooth (as her regular vet thought), but the teeth rubbing together has caused a hole to form in her gum. The teeth also rubbed some of the bone away. The more he talks, the more I wince.

After several minutes of medical gobble gook, Dr. Moore explains the options for correcting the problem in layman's terms. One option even includes braces. *Is Sally going to wear a retainer?* Dr. Moore thinks Sally is a little old for braces. After we review the options, I ask what he would do with his dog in this situation. And that is what I choose.

We discuss the cost—yikes!—and I gave him my approval to go ahead.

I call Mike.

"Sally update," he says, instead of hello.

I sniffle.

"Is she okay?"

"Yeah, but she has a malocclusion degeneration."

"Malo what?"

"That's what I said." I repeat most of what Dr. Moore told me, along with the plan of action and the cost.

"Yikes," Mike says.

"I know."

"Call me when you hear back from the doctor. And don't worry; she's going to be okay."

Later that afternoon, Dr. Moore calls to say everything is done and Sally is fine. I breathe a BIG sigh of relief, one I didn't realize I had been holding all day.

I call Mike.

"Sally update," he demands.

"She is doing well." I lean back in my chair. "Dr. Moore said there were no surprises and everything went the way he expected. "

I hear Mike let out a sigh.

"I'll pick her up in a few hours."

"Call me when you get her."

When I show up at the dental vet office later that afternoon, I am again greeted with smiles and reassurances from the staff.

"Sally is so sweet."

"Sally is such a good dog."

Dr. Moore shows me photos of Sally's mouth and teeth. They look awful.

"See," Dr. Moore says, pointing. "Here is where the bone has been rubbed off."

He points to the place where he performed a coronal reduction. My eyes must have crossed so he takes out a fake dog mouth thingy and shows me how the canines were rubbing against each other, and how they won't anymore.

"Do you think this was causing her any pain?"

"Yes."

Bad doggy mom guilt sucks me up like a vacuum cleaner and I feel my shoulders droop. How can this be? Sally has been in all this pain and we didn't know? I can almost hear the Animal Protective Services revving their motors as they tear toward my house, handcuffs at the ready.

"Can I see her?" I ask.

"Oh sure, she's right over there."

Across the room, Sally is listing to one side in a kennel.

I scoop her into my arms, nuzzle her neck and shower her face with kisses. She nestles into me, as much as a muscular twenty-nine pound dog can nestle, and I feel better.

As I head toward the door, several technicians reach out to scratch Sally's head and talk to her. In the car, I strap her into her purple harness. She curls into the seat and rests her head on the arm rest.

I call Mike.

"Sally update," he says.

"Good news and bad news," I say. "Good news, she's a little woozy, but otherwise she seems to be doing fine." I scratch her ear and she closes her eyes.

"And the bad news?"

"The vet says no more dragging the garden rake around the yard."

"Sally is not going to like that," he says. " Not one bit."

Say Ahh!

A Disaster in Dog-sitting

I have offered to dog-sit my daughter's new puppy and it is an unbelievable nightmare, for all of us. Lyle (yes, Lyle) is a three-month-old rescue puppy. He looks like he has some shepherd in him and perhaps a little giraffe also, as his legs are very, very long. And he might have a little Jell-o in there too, because he doesn't seem to have bones. It is very strange.

Anyway, it is 5:30 a.m. and Lyle is standing by the front door whining and whining and whining. I know he needs to go outside but I am soooooooo tired that I don't care if he poops or pees by the front door, as long as he does it quietly. But he is not quiet.

I get up and let him out. He pees and runs back in. I get settled into bed and he is back at the door, whining. I get up and let him out AGAIN. He poops and runs back in. Now, of course, I am wide awake and so are Sally and Mary.

I lie in bed and stare at the ceiling for an hour and then get up. Lyle is jumping on every dog and cat in the house, trying to get someone to play with him. They do not find him amusing.

I'm getting ready for work in the bathroom and when I look into the bedroom, Sally and Mary are sitting in the middle of the bed staring at me. And it isn't a look of adoration. It is more like, "what the heck?!" Lyle is chewing the on the edge of the bedspread because he can't get onto the bed.

"Sorry guys," I say.

Sally jumps off the bed and comes into the bathroom. Lyle is jumping on her head and biting her ears. Think of a baboon, you know, one of those primates that have colorful faces. Now think of their noses, long with odd wrinkles. That is what Sally has looked like the past few days. Her lips are always sneering, which makes her nose wrinkle.

Sally stands between my legs, which I realize is a calculated move on her part. That way, when Lyle is jumping on her head he is also jumping on my feet and nipping my ankles.

"Ow!" I look down and I swear Sally is smiling at me.

When I'm ready to leave, I shove Lyle into his kennel. We are in no way leaving him out while we're gone because I'm afraid the dogs will tie him up and the cats will perform torture on him. I leave for work and return several hours later. Mary meets me at the back door. Lyle is barking and whining, excited to get out of his prison.

I walk into my bedroom and am hit with a really, really bad smell. Poop! I glance around and Sally is next to her kennel with her paw over her nose.

Lyle has pooped diarrhea all over the bed in his kennel. Oh no! I take the bed to the laundry room and wipe up the slimy stuff with a tissue, gagging like crazy. Big gags! I lean over the toilet to throw the last tissue in there and I puke. Seriously! Thank goodness I was already leaning over the toilet. But my puke stuff is red ... OMG its blood. No, wait. I drank that cherry slushy on the way home.

I put the bed into the washer and hear a commotion in the living room. Lyle has Stan, the cat, pinned behind the table and he is wrapped around the lamp cord, which is about to pull the lamp from the table.

I wrestle Lyle away from Stan and open the door. "Okay everybody, out!"

Mary and Sally dash through the door with Lyle close on their heels. I sit on the chair on the front porch and breathe a sigh of relief.

Until I notice Lyle rolling in something in the woods.

A Playmate for Sally

"Sally needs a playmate," I say.

"No way will the princess want another dog taking attention from her," Mike responds. "Besides, Sally can play with Mary."

"Mary just chases her ball and sleeps on her pillow. Anyway, I saw this really interesting dog in the last issue of <u>Cats and Dogs Magazine</u>." I open it to the Wishbone Pet Rescue page and show Mike.

Eli - 1.5 year. Cattle Dog/Jack Russell Mix. Hi, I'm Eli.
I'm looking for a home with a JOB. How about a small
lap dog that will excel at agility? I stand 12" at my shoulders.
I run faster than anyone. I also love to cuddle in bed.

"His JOB will be to play with Sally," I say.

"A Jack Russell and Australian cattle dog? Do you know how much energy he is going to have?"

I submit an internet application to Wishbone, and a week or so later Eli and four of his caretakers come for a visit.

The cars pull into the driveway and Eli jumps out.

"Hi, Eli." I bend over and let him smell my hand. Sally and Mary are conducting a sniff-a-thon while Eli turns in a circle, trying to sniff them back.

He runs around in the back yard, Mary walks with her ball in her mouth, and Sally does her happy spinning. I bend to pet Eli and he bounces straight up in the air, smacking my nose with his head.

"Well, I can see the Jack Russell in him," I say, rubbing my nose. Eli takes off running and Sally darts after him. Mike sits on the porch and smiles. If Mike were Sally he would be doing the happy spin right now.

"This might actually work," Mike says as he tosses Mary's ball.

Eli runs to Mary and jumps at her in play. Mary gives him a lip sneer and Eli backs away. Sally and Eli never exchange one snarl during the visit.

A few weeks later, Eli comes for a sleepover per Wishbone policy. He arrives on a Friday. Eli and Sally chase each other inside the house and outside in the yard. When they scrap with each other, Eli goes for the back of Sally's legs, which is difficult because she is often spinning.

We stack Eli's kennel on top of Sally's in our bedroom and he bounces in and out. The first night he gets into his kennel when we go to bed. During the night he gets out of his kennel several times and jumps onto our bed. He sniffs us and then goes back to his kennel. It is as if he is checking to make sure we are still there.

The weekend is a success. Eli stays in the yard when he is outside, and comes when called. At the end of the weekend we talk to Wishbone and the adoption is approved. Eli has a new forever home and Sally has a playmate.

Then things start to change. That night Eli is in and out of his kennel as usual, and although it was adorable the first night, being woken up all night is not amusing. And every time he gets out of his kennel, Sally scrambles out from under the covers and bashes into my face. We spend a very restless night.

When we let him outside the next day, Eli takes off into the woods. I panic because I can't see him.

"Eli, here!" I yell. But no Eli. I'm really panicking when he flies around the pole barn. Later, we attach a bell to his collar so we can hear him.

Then he lifts a leg and pees on the wall in the hallway.

"He was on his best behavior over the weekend," Mike says, "and now that he knows he is in, he is being naughty."

With loving, yet stern, discipline, Eli calms down. He still races around in the woods, but he comes when called.

At night, both dogs jump into our bed and settle in. It is soothing to have a dog snuggled against my body, until I wake up and Sally is smashed against my left side and Eli is on my right. I can't move for the entire night.

"We should lock Eli in his kennel tonight," I say as we get ready for bed the next evening. Sally is already under the covers.

"That's not fair," Mike says. "Sally gets to sleep in the bed with us."

"Please, I'm begging you," I whine. "We have to do something. I need sleep."

"Eli, kennel," Mike says. Eli hops into his kennel and snuggles into his pillow. Mike locks the door and shuts off the light. "I can't look at him."

"Why not?"

"Because I know he's staring at me."

"Don't be silly," I say. "He's probably already asleep."

Mike climbs into bed and just as I am about to drift off to sleep, I hear it.

"Did you hear that?" Mike says. "He's crying."

"Let him out." I sigh. "Sleep is overrated anyway."

Sally's Water Adventure

I run through the rain and hand a plastic tub of clothes to Mike. He arranges it in the back of the truck as I run back to the garage and grab a bin of food. We play this back-and-forth game until everything has been loaded: doggy stuff, our bicycles, kayaks, canoe and cooler. Next, I stuff the dog pillows into the back seat and arrange them into comfy nesting places for the five-hour ride to Bois Blanc Island, our vacation destination. When we are ready to leave, I strap the little white dog and her brother, Eli, into the seatbelts. Eli curls into a ball and Sally starts trying to chew her way out of the harness.

"Sally, quit already," I say.

When we arrive at the rental cottage, we tumble out of the truck and stretch, even Sally and Eli. After that, Eli starts checking the perimeter of the area, looking for rodents to chase. Sally wanders over to the porch and sits. We unload everything and walk down to Lake Huron, which is right behind the cottage.

We were here last summer and even though we tried and tried, Sally refused to go into the lake. She wouldn't get close enough to even get her paws wet. At home, I took her to dog parks and she refused to go near the ponds. I bought a kiddie pool, filled it with clean water and put her in it. She stood statue-like, as if the water was cement. So we know how Sally is going to act, but we wonder how Eli is going to react.

We walk into the lake and Eli follows behind. We keep walking and so does he. When the water gets to his tummy, he takes a quick step backwards and runs into Sally. Sally? Really? She has followed Eli into the lake.

"Mike, Sally's in the water."

"No way."

"Way."

Mike spins around, causing a little splashing and that does it. Sally runs back to the shore.

The next day, we put the canoe into the lake. Mike wants to take Eli out in it and see how he reacts. His dream is that he will be able to take Eli on canoeing trips with him. We put Eli's doggy life jacket on him, a snappy blue and grey combo, and Mike picks him up by the top strap. Eli hangs in the air, his paws making a swimming movement. We put him in the front of the canoe and Mike starts paddling. I'm enjoying the view of them floating out in the lake when out of the corner of my eye I see Sally swimming past me. Seems she wants to go canoeing, too.

I am stunned but manage to grab at her. I stumble on the rocky bottom and steady myself by sticking one arm into the water. I make a grab at her with my other arm. She pulls against me, but I'm able to get both of us back to shore without falling.

Sally stands on the bank, whimpering and watching our guys in the boat.

A few minutes later, they return. Mike gets out into the shallow water and pulls the boat to shore where Eli jumps out and runs to Sally. She licks his head.

"Sally was trying to follow you," I say.

"Get out."

"No, really. She swam right past me and I had to drag her back to shore."

"Let's see how she does in the kayak," Mike says. He takes the life jacket off Eli and puts it on Sally. Again with the cement act. She doesn't move.

I settle into the kayak, and Mike carries her out and puts her in with me. I think it's going to work as she sits looking out at the water. Then she stands, and the kayak starts wobbling from side to side.

"This is so not working," I say. She puts her front paws on the edge and the kayak leans dangerously. Mike grabs the boat as I step out, once again stumbling on the rock bottom. I am headed toward a face full of water when Mike grabs my arm. He has to let go of the kayak and Sally takes this opportunity to jump out. Mike saves me from a dunk in the lake and Sally gets to the shore and has a full body shake. Without looking back, she makes a beeline to the cottage.

"I think that's the end of Sally's kayaking adventures," I say.

She's standing on the deck and staring at the door of the cottage. "Yeah, I think that's a pretty safe bet," Mike says. "Maybe tomorrow we can give her a ride in the canoe."

"Good luck with that," I say.

The Great Outdoors

Mary found a garter snake in the backyard and when she bent to take a closer look, it lunged and bit her on the nose. I say bit, but the snake's mouth could not open wide enough to bite her. Mary didn't flinch. She cocked her head in that way dogs do. She bent closer to the snake and it struck her again. That was enough for Mary and she walked away.

Sally found a garter snake in the grass once. She lay down by it and focused those little black eyes on the poor creature. When it started moving, she leapt straight up into the air. If it had struck at Sally, I don't know what she would have done, but I know she would not have just walked away.

Sally enjoys stalking toads in the yard. If you can define stalking as staring at an amphibian without moving a muscle. Once again, if the toad jumps, Sally leaps. Not at the toad, but away from it.

Then there is Eli. He is not afraid. While we were vacationing on Bois Blanc Island, Eli would run the perimeter of the yard, looking for intruders. Those intruders were often chipmunks and squirrels. While he was doing his job, Sally was doing her job of basking in the sun or waiting to be let back inside.

One morning the dogs didn't come back to the door as usual after I called for them. I wandered outside and heard a squirrel chattering up a storm. He was not happy. I walked around the pine trees and discovered the reason for his displeasure. Eli and Sally were sitting at the bottom of a tree and staring up at the squirrel who was sitting on a branch. I called to them, but they didn't even turn their heads. Once Sally broke the stare and looked at Eli before she resumed her sentry position. Every day after that, as soon as the dogs were outside they would run to the tree and stare into the branches.

Mike was blowing leaves at home the other day. All the dogs were outside with him when he saw Eli and Mary staring at something on the ground. The something moved and the dogs moved. Mike walked over and saw a poor little mouse panting. He reached toward it and Eli snatched it into his mouth.

"Eli, drop that," Mike said. Eli looked up at him with the mouse's tail hanging out of his mouth. He was not eating the mouse, just holding it in his jaws.

Mike moved toward him. Eli turned and went flying around the side of the house. The chase was on. Mary was running behind Eli and Mike was behind Mary. When they passed Sally, who was lying on the porch, she joined the chase. Mike turned the corner and there was Eli, but no mouse.

"You don't think he ate it, do you?" Mike asked me when I got home

An involuntary shiver ran down my body. "I don't want to even think about it," I said. "But I would think twice before you let him lick you in the face today."

At that moment, Sally came around the house munching on something.

"You don't think?" I asked.

"Sally, drop," Mike said.

And our courageous little hunter spit out an acorn.

No Dogs Allowed

On Saturday, our real estate agent held an open house at our home. We spent the morning cleaning and trying to make the house look devoid of canine inhabitants. That means the bowls went into the cabinet in the garage, the blankets and doggy pillows went into the crates, and the crates went into the garage.

But what would we do with the dogs? We could put them in their crates in the garage. Yeah, like that is going to happen. NOT!

We gather them in the garage with their harnesses in hand. Sally and Eli love to see the harnesses because they love to get in the car. However, they are not much help in getting into the harness. Eli starts out standing and ends up sprawled on his back on the garage floor in a melted dirty snow puddle. Sally is so excited she is spinning like a whirling dervish. It is hard to strap her in when she's twirling at a maddening speed. But with determination and a bit of begging, we get them both harnessed, literally. Mary has never worn a harness, and when we approached her with one, she panicked. At 12 years old, (that is about 69 in human years), it would be a little stressful to introduce her to a harness now.

Maneuvering the dogs into harnesses is only a small part of this procedure. Next, we open the car doors and they storm in. They enter through opposite doors and almost bang their heads together when they reach the middle of the back seat. We wrestle them into the seatbelts and Mary takes her spot sitting between the duo. Mike and I are already exhausted, yet the adventure has just begun.

We drive to a nearby park to let them run, play and wear themselves out. At our destination, Mike gets out and opens the car doors. The pooches leap out into the snow. I button my coat all the way up to my neck, wrap my scarf around my face, adjust my earmuffs and put on my gloves. By the time I get out of the car, Mike and the dogs are halfway down the path.

"Hey, wait for me." I walk/shuffle/run after them and try not to slip in the snow. Sally bounds toward looking like a giant bunny making huge hippity-hops through the deep snow. She disappears with every down hop. When she reaches me, she turns and watches Eli running toward us at full speed. This is an invitation for scrappin' and she pounces after him. They meet in a tangle, then separate and chase each other again.

Mary is running ahead, oblivious to the young-uns and their mischief. Or maybe she's just annoyed with them. When she starts to get too far away from us, Mike calls and calls and calls after her. She seems to be developing selective hearing. I had a grandmother with that once. She could not hear you unless you whispered; then she heard you just fine.

Once Mike gets Mary's attention, he pats his knees and she starts galloping toward us. She runs half in and half out of the snow banks lining the path. She even puts her head down in the fluffy snow as she runs. She looks like a doggy snow-plow. When she is this active and happy, it is difficult to imagine she is well into her senior years.

Back and forth, we walk the dogs down the empty snowy road. Sally runs full blast into a snow bank and her head disappears. Mary finds something of interest in the snow and stuffs her head straight down. They look like headless creatures.

"Where's Eli?" I ask.

Mike points at my feet. Eli is walking close at my heels, herding me along. This little man has a job to do and he does it well. We have to coax him into playing a bit more.

"Can we go home yet?" Mike asks.

I check my watch and hurray! We can head back to the house. The one-hour open house should be wrapping up. We head to the car and Sally beats us there, running from one door to the other. We open the doors and three snowy dogs jump in. Sally decides this would be a good time to shake, as does Mary. Little snowballs fly around inside the car. Of course, the shaking could not occur before they got in the car. What fun would that have been?

Everyone is quiet and subdued on the ride back to the house, except for Sally. While Mary and Eli lay their heads on their paws and close their eyes, Sally gives me the Sally stink eye because I won't let her sit on my lap. And it is not pretty.

At the house, we put everything back in its proper place. Mary nestles into her chair, and it doesn't take long before two little tired doggies snuggle together in front of the fireplace. Life is good.

Whose Bed Is It Anyway?

"Seriously, Sally?" I lift my head from the pillow and squint at the alarm clock. 2:31 a.m. Wednesday. Sally nudges my arm again with her long snout. I swing my legs out of the covers while Sally lands with a thump on the floor.

This is the second time she has woken me to go outside, and I am less than happy. I feel with my toes before standing on the floor so I don't step on Mary. She is napping on her pillow beside the bed. Eli snoozes in his kennel, and Mike is snoring over on his side of the bed.

"Why don't you ever wake up your dad?" I whisper to the little white dog at my feet.

As I open the front door against the wind, Sally dashes through my legs and out into the snow. I close the door and scratch the frost off the glass so I can keep an eye on her. She wanders, sniffing at every deviation in the snow banks. I pull my hands inside my pajamas to keep warm and continue to watch. As soon as she squats, I open the door.

"Come on, ya little brat." She looks at the door, and then wanders toward the side yard. "Sally!" She stops, looks at me over her shoulder, then turns and bounds back to the house. Bounding at 2:30 a.m.? Who does that?

She is snuggled under the covers before I even get back into the bed and is such dead weight that I find myself arranging my body around hers. When did this become her bed?

Before we got Sally, I went online and read several articles about dog training. They all said the same thing; do not let your dog sleep with you. Ha! This had never worked with any of our other dogs, but I was determined to do the right thing with this puppy. On Sally's first night, I put her kennel next to the bed, tucked her inside and turned off the light. Silence. This was so easy. I closed my eyes and odd little alien noises started emanating from the doggy container.

"What is that?" Mike asked.

"I think it's Sally."

"No, really, what is it?"

We listened. Sure enough, it was Sally. Not a whine, whimper, or bark. This was a sound unlike any I had ever heard from a dog before. Come to think of it, unlike any I had heard period. I thumped the top of the kennel with my knuckle. "Quiet." That is what the dog articles had said to do.

The noise stopped and I settled back into my pillows.

"What if I scared her when I thumped?" I whispered to Mike.

"She's fine."

Quiet.

"I feel ..."

The noise started again.

"That does it," I said. I leaned over the edge, opened the kennel and scooped up the pig-like puppy. Mike held the back of my pajamas so I wouldn't fall out of bed.

"Okay, pull," I said. He pulled me up and I put Sally between us. She licked Mike's face, turned around twice and settled under the blankets. Thus, the bedtime routine was established.

Now I lift my arm and hold up the blankets as the white dog emerges. She lays her head on the pillow beside mine. I open my eyes and she is staring at me. It is unnerving so I roll over and she starts stretching her legs, which means kicking, which means her paws are battering against my back. This is not conducive to a restful sleep.

"That's it," I say as I throw back the blankets. Sally jumps up and body shakes. She leaps off the bed and heads for the door. "Sally, kennel."

She stops, and then takes a tentative step forward.

"Sally, kennel," I repeat. She turns, walks back to the bed and jumps up. I wrap her in my arms and carry her to the kennel. In the dark, I stub my toe on the bedpost and utter a few unhappy words. I set her in front of the kennel and give her a little shove. She stands solid.

Now understand, Sally loves her kennel. It's fancy with a gigantic pillow inside that makes it a warm nesting place. During the day, she will go inside just to nap. So going into her kennel is not a bad thing. Except for tonight, it seems.

"Sally, in." I give her another little shove and she walks inside. I close and lock the door, limp back to bed and nestle into the blankets. I hear her turn around a couple of times and plop into the pillows with a loud yawn.

Five hours later, my alarm goes off. It is amazing. Sally has not made a peep and even now, she is quiet. In fact, I think she is snoring.

"I think Sally should start sleeping in her kennel every night," I whisper to Mike.

"Um hmm," he says. "Like that's going to happen."

"No, really. This is going to be the new bedtime routine."

"Right."

"Seriously, Sally?"

The little dog nudges my arm with her snout as I lift my head and look at the clock.

2:18 a.m. Thursday.

Life With Sally

The Book Thief

The sound of paper ripping makes me pause as I brush my teeth. I cock my head toward the bathroom door. *What is that?*

My mind goes over the items in my bedroom in rapid fire--bed, blanket, rug, fan, pillows, paperback book on bedside table--oh no! I spit, throw my toothbrush on the counter and rush to Eli's kennel. Sure enough. He gives me his guilty "who me?" look, and there is something peeking out from behind him. My new book, minus the cover, which I find tucked between his front paws.

"Eli," I say. "Really? You're such a little thief." I snatch the book and put it away.

Bright light bursts into the room and a rumble of thunder follows. Eli explodes from his kennel and runs into the kitchen, around the table and back into the bedroom. His eyes are frantic as he scans the room. His terror is palpable.

I climb into bed and pat the blanket beside me. He takes one leap and lands, trembling, yet sitting erect. I rub his ears and pull him in close to me.

"It's okay, Eli," I whisper. He lies on his side, but stays alert.

I think back to the weather forecast I heard earlier in the day--thunderstorms all night.This is going to be a long night. I reach around Eli with the hand that isn't patting him and turn off the light. I curl on my side, wrapping him into me with both arms and his body relaxes.

Mike is gone for the night so it's just me and the doggies. Sally jumps up on the other side of the bed, then scootches under the covers and drops against me with a thud. I'm wedged between two dogs and can't move. Did I say it was going to be a long night?

As I start to doze off, more lightning flashes. Not good. Little Eli's body tenses and I whisper my mantra of "it's okay," over and over. I rub his side and pull him even closer. As the thunder rumbles and the window panes shake, he burrows into me, but he's not trembling. It's working! I relax a bit. Then Sally pops her head out from under the covers.

Sally has never shown concern over thunderstorms or loud noises. But she is concerned when we change her food bowls. She is concerned if the refrigerator door is open and she wants to walk past it. And she is concerned if the cats are watching her when she eats. But loud noises and thunderstorms, no problem. Until tonight. My guess is that she sees the attention Eli is getting and figures she wants in on it, too.

I have rolled to my back by this time and she crawls across my stomach and stops. Her head and front legs are on one side of my body and her back legs on the other. And she is no lightweight. I am about to push her off when I see her lean in the direction of Eli and stretch her head toward him. I wait for her to bite his ear because that is how they play, but she doesn't. With a subtle, quiet movement she rests her chin on the top of his head. Awwwwwwwwwww!

I'm surprised by her gentleness and want us to stay like this, but my stomach is really starting to hurt from Sally's bony, heavy body. I'm going to have to move her, even though I don't want to disturb this moment of extreme cuteness. A sudden flash of lightning does it for me.

Sally scrambles backward off my body. Eli leaps from the bed. Sally chases after him as he runs out of the room and into the kitchen. I follow their movements by the sound of their paws scrabbling against the floor. Mary jumps up from her pillow and stumbles to the door just as the other two run back in. There is a mini collision as the three dogs fall into and around each other. More thunder rumbles and Eli runs into the closet, Sally following close behind. She's trying to bite his ear. This is nuts!

I look at the clock: 11:30 p.m. I did say this was going to be a long night, didn't I?

I get up and gather Sally and Eli back into my bed. I call Mary and she drops onto her pillow. My doggy bookends snuggle into me and once again I start to drift off — until I hear an odd sound. *What is that chewing noise?* I listen closely, sigh and reach around to Eli's mouth.

"Drop it," I say and he spits out a gob of my paperback.

Don't Leave Us Behind

I grunt as I carry a box of kitchen stuff and put it into the back of my Honda. A slight movement in the front seat catches my attention. Lifting up onto my toes, I peer into the car. *What is he doing in there?* I think.

"Eli?" I say. He looks at me, and then ducks his head below the seat. Since he has shown a propensity toward eating anything he can find, even those things not edible, I run to the driver's door and fling it open.

"What do you have this time, you little rascal?"

He's on the floor between the driver's seat and the pedals, and when he sees me, he ducks again. I feel on the floor all around him and find nothing. So what he is doing here and why does he keep trying to hide? Hiding in the car? Okay, now I get it.

"Don't worry, Eli," I say. "We're not going to leave you behind."

We are in the process of moving and it is a nightmare. Exhaustion has replaced our earlier excitement of buying the house. It is difficult to remain enthusiastic as you pack the

900th box, carry it to the car, drive to the new house, carry it in, and then unpack it.

Everyday while Mike is at work, I make two to three trips to the new house with a car full of boxes, bins, bags, and clothes. And while I'm packing and moving, the dogs are watching and, I can only presume, wondering what the heck is going on.

I lean into the car and give Eli a scratch on the head.

"Come on buddy, out of the car."

He jumps out and follows me into the house where I pick up another box. I head back to the garage and when Sally weaves between my legs, I stumble and the box of pans crashes to the floor. Doggy nails scrabble on the floor behind me and as I look over my shoulder, I see her tail as she flies into the other room with Eli close on her heels. I sink to the floor and rest my forehead on my knees. I am exhausted, my feet hurt, and pots and pans that need to be re-packed surround me. As I sit in my self-imposed pity, I feel a snout nudging my elbow. It is a little white snout. A tiny bit of lovin' from Sally is just what I need. I give her a hug and get back to work.

The week continues in a blur of the same--packing, carrying, driving, carrying, and unpacking. On one occasion, the dogs run around outside as I walk in and out of the old house.

"Okay guys, back inside," I say.

Eli and Mary bound past me, then stop and wait for their treat. I look out the door and see Sally walking toward the house at a snail's pace.

"Come on, Sal."

When she gets to the car, she pauses, then stops and gazes at the driver's door. She looks at me, then back at the car. At me, at the car. This continues for several minutes.

"How about a treat, Sally?"

Food is often a good motivator for Sally. Not this time. She just stares at the car, then me. You get the pattern. I walk out and scoop her into my arms.

"Soon, Sally, soon you'll be going to the new house with me."

Today we make the final move and will start living at the new house. All the furniture and boxes are there, and it is time to bring the doggies.

"Hey guys, ready to go for a ride?" A mini herd of fur barrels past me and out to the open doors of the car. Mary hops in and jumps into the back seat. Sally and Eli jump in at the same time and collide.

"They are going to love the new house," I say to Mike as we make the 10-minute drive.

"And the pond," he reminds me.

"Oh, the pond. That has mess written all over it. Maybe we should keep them away until we have doggy towels by the back door."

"Like that's going to happen." He snickers as he pulls into the driveway and parks.

I open the back door; the dogs jump out and make a beeline for the water.

"Wait, wait," I say, but it is useless. Sally has startled a frog and she is up to her tummy in the water searching for it. Looks like she will be doing a bit of frog licking this summer. Eli is splashing along the bank and Mary is sitting and perusing everything.

"Where are the doggy towels?" I ask.

Mike points to the huge array of boxes filling the garage.

"In one of those," he says.

The Strawberry Bandit

Strawberries with ice cream. Strawberries with short-bread. Strawberries with pudding. But strawberries and a little white dog?

Mike and I moved in May and as we were walking around the property, we noticed a strawberry patch--a large strawberry patch. Not too long after our discovery, it was covered with white flowers, and after that lots and lots of green berries.

Today as I look out the window, I spot a few ripe red strawberries. I grab a bowl and head to the patch with three doggies following along. I swat at a couple mosquitoes and the closer we get, the thicker the swarm surrounding me grows. I look down and my legs are peppered with their dark, flighty, stinging bodies.

"Aaaaaaaahhhhhhhhh," I scream as I run back to the garage. I grab the nearest can of bug spray and douse every inch of bare skin, then give a quick spray to my clothes, just in case. My entourage and I venture forth again.

Mary leads the way and once inside the fenced area, she digs up a dirt patch and curls into it. Eli and Sally walk right into the strawberries. I start picking at one end. After several minutes, I stand to stretch my back.

Strawberry plants are flying behind Eli as he digs a hole in the patch.

"Eli, no digging," I call to him.

Sally has her face buried in the leaves searching for toads. At least I think she is toad hunting until she lifts her head and I spot the stem of a strawberry hanging out of her mouth. I laugh as she dips her head back in and I hear chomping.

I continue picking and soon she is alongside me munching away. I chuckle until I look down and see a tan spider the size of Florida on her back. Its legs are about 10 feet long and its body is hairy and scary. Sally gazes at me with that silly grin of hers. I flinch as I brush my hand at the monster hitching a ride on her back, but I miss. I'm not sure how I miss something that huge, but I do.

"Eeeeeeeeee, Sally," I say. I jump backwards as I slap at the gargantuan beast and it flies away from me. I shudder and put on my garden gloves before I continue picking.

A few days later, my friend, Janet, comes over. I don't tell her about the spider but I do offer her a pair of gloves. She has brought her own so maybe she is aware of the danger lurking.

"Sally likes to eat the strawberries," I say as we start picking. I grab a large, juicy, perfect strawberry. "Look at this one." I turn it around and find a big bite taken out of it.

"Wonder who did this?" I look at the little white dog that is neck deep in the plants.

My back is to Janet as we move around the berry patch.

"Hey Sally, that's mine," Janet says. I turn and see a face-off as Sally and Janet head toward the same berry.

Janet grabs Sally's ball and throws it across the yard. Sally ignores it and continues strawberry hunting.

My sister, Joyce, shows up and starts filling her pint containers.

"Sally, get out of there," she says.

"What happened?" I ask.

"I turned around and Sally had her nose in my container," she says. "I reached for the bowl and she grabbed a berry and took off."

Sally is stretched out in the berries, giving us her best innocent look. The red around her mouth is a dead giveaway though. Our picking continues.

"Hey," Joyce says. "You little snot!"

"Now what?" I ask. Sally is standing in front of her.

"She snatched that berry right out of my hand."

"Get out!"

"I'm serious."

Later that evening I am on the couch with Sally burrowed in beside me when Joyce calls.

"Thanks for the strawberries," she says. "And thanks to Sally I found another partially eaten one in my bowl."

"Picking strawberries must be exhausting for her, because she is sacked out beside me right now. She's really cute, except for the smell emanating from her."

"Must be the strawberries. Lucky you."

I hold my breath and fan the air over Sally's rear. "Yeah, lucky me."

Life With Sally

Not the Doggy Door!

Two doggy doors! One from kitchen to garage, and the other from garage to outside dog run. I'm salivating with happiness. No more taking Sally outside in the middle of the night as she can take herself out. And no more poop surprises when I'm gone too long during the day.

"Mike, I forgot about the doggy doors," I say. "This is great."

"You don't really think Sally is ever going through those doors, do you?" He laughs.

"Yes. It's just going to take a bit of creative encouragement."

"Okay, here is my prediction."

Here we go. Mike is full of predictions and they are often correct, which is really infuriating. "Well?"

"Eli is going to learn to use the doors first, and then Mary. Sally is never going near them."

"You're wrong."

Mike leaves the room and I start doubting my prediction. The truth is, Sally doesn't like new things. She refuses to go near her new dish and even barks at it. How am I going to get her to go through a swinging door?

I start my project a few days later while Mike is at work, with the kitchen/garage doggy door. I duct tape the swinging part of the door open, then crouch on the garage side and call the dogs. Eli runs over and looks at me. Mary stands behind him. Sally stays across the room in the bedroom doorway, on the carpet. She is not too keen about the hardwood floor, yet.

"Come on, Eli," I say, holding out a treat. He jumps through the door.

Mary takes a few steps closer and sniffs every edge.

"Come on, Mary." She steps through the door one dainty paw at a time. I give her a treat.

Eli runs through the door, turns and runs back again. "Don't be a show off, Eli." I hear a little whine and see Sally still standing on the bedroom carpeting, her tail wagging.

"Come on, Sal." No movement.

I crawl closer to the opening, dragging my knees across the cement threshold. "Ouch."

Sally takes one tentative step onto the hardwood floor. "Good girl." She steps back.

I stick my head and shoulders through the doggy opening. "Come on." Two steps forward, then three steps back.

Laughing comes from behind me and I bang my head as I back out of the door.

"What are you doing?" my sister Kendra asks. She has come to pick strawberries.

I squat on my heels and rub my head. "Trying to get Sally to come through."

"Hi Sally," Kendra says.

Sally wags her tail and takes a couple careful steps forward.

"Come on," I say. All four paws are now on the hardwood and she is moving closer, albeit with great care.

Eli rushes past Kendra and through the door. Sally runs backwards, paws slipping and sliding. Eli jumps back out.

"You're not being much of a helpy-helper, Eli," I say. I put a rug in front of the doggy door on the kitchen side. Back in the garage, I crawl halfway through again.

"Come on, Sal. We can't let Mike be right."

After about 10 minutes, she has managed to come across the scary hardwood floor to the rug. I give her a treat, then back out of the door.

"You can do it," I say. She sits. "Come on, Sal-mal." She leans forward without moving her paws as I reach a treat closer to the door. Her snout reaches the treat and as she grabs it, she backs up, her paws hit the hardwood and she slips, feet scrambling beneath her.

"This is so not working."

"Do you have better treats?" Kendra asks.

"We should find some toads and she could lick them."

Kendra laughs so hard she snorts. I stick my hand through the opening and when Sally steps towards me, I take hold of her collar.

"Come on, Sal, its okay." I lead her closer to the door and with a gentle pull; she steps through one tentative paw at a time.

I wrap her in a big hug, stand and give Kendra a high-five. We do a happy dance with Eli jumping at our feet and Sally spinning circles. Mary is sleeping in a patch of sunlight.

Inside the house, I crouch and call Sally through the doggy door. She steps in with no hesitation.

"You are so smart," I say. I grab the phone as Kendra coaxes her back outside with a treat.

"Guess what Sally is doing, Mr. Doubting Doubter?" I ask when Mike answers the phone.

"Barking at her dish again? Quaking at the sight of the hardwood floor?"

"She is jumping back and forth through that doggy door like it's nothing." I smile.

"No way."

"Way!"

At that moment, Eli leaps through the door behind Sally. Her feet go out from under her and she starts running in place on the hardwood floor. Her legs are moving, but she isn't going anywhere. Then she skates across the kitchen to the safety of the bedroom carpet.

"What was that noise?" Mike asks.

"Oh, nothing," I say. "Gotta go." I hang up and peek into the bedroom. Her majesty is lying in a pile of pillows on the bed. I think her doggy door days may be done.

Compassionate Sally

I climb into bed and pull the comforter up to my chin.

"Where's Sally?" Mike asks.

"You're not going to believe this," I say. "She's in bed with Cathy."

"You're kidding me."

"Do I sound like I'm kidding? That little dog is a brat." Eli leaps out of his kennel and snuggles next to me. "You're a good boy, aren't you Eli."

"I can't believe she's blowing you off," Mike says.

"Believe it." I pull Eli closer to me.

It started earlier that evening with a call from my girlfriend, Cathy. She was having relationship problems and wanted to stay overnight. We spent the evening on the living room couch talking and watching bad television. Eli snuggled up on my right and Sally scooted in between Cathy and me on my left. At 10:00 p.m., after half an hour of yawning, we said good night to each other. I headed to my bedroom, expecting Sally would follow behind as usual. When I noticed she wasn't there, I walked back to the guest room. Sally was sitting on the bed.

"Come on, Sal," I said. "Let's go to bed." The bed word always works, except this time. She didn't move.

Cathy shrugged. "She's okay in here."

What? Sleep without Sally? I thought. *Are you nuts?* "Well, if she bugs you too much, just kick her out and shut your door."

I gave it one more try and patted my leg. "Come on Sal."

"Really, she's fine." Cathy wrapped her arm around Sally and scratched behind her ear. Sally, with great drama, fell into her lap.

In the morning, Mike showers and dresses for work. When he is in the kitchen, I hear the tap tap tapping of Sally's nails on the hardwood floor.

"Where have you been, you little traitor?" Mike says.

She runs into our bedroom and leaps onto the bed. After licking me several times on the face, she scoots underneath the blankets. Finally. I sigh, smile and close my eyes, ready for a little more sleep with my snuggler. Sally has other ideas. She bolts out from under the covers and dives off the bed. I hear her paws on the floor as she heads back to Cathy's bedroom.

An hour later, Eli is nudging me to go out. I open the front door and he runs outside, followed by her highness, who has deigned to join us. After the outside business is over, Eli and Sally run back into the house. She turns to the left and into the room where Cathy is now watching Good Morning America. I sit on the bed beside her. Sally is between us when I sit down, but within minutes, she is on Cathy's lap. *Really, Sally?* I pull her over to me and scratch her tummy. As soon as I stop, she is back on Cathy's lap.

I'm getting a wee bit annoyed and not understanding this at all. Cathy has been over before and Sally has never acted like this. In fact, Sally has never spent the night in any bed other than ours.

The phone rings. "Hello?"

"Is Sally still blowing you off?" Mike asks.

"Yes."

He laughs.

"I don't get it," I say. "I've never seen her act like this."

"Maybe she's tuning into Cathy's emotions and knows she needs comforting right now."

That would be a big stretch for Sally, but I toss the idea around in my head for a few minutes. I know dogs can be very cued into our emotions, so maybe Mike is right.

"Awwwww," I say. "I bet you're right. How sweet is that?"

I hang up and give Sally a big hug.

"You're such a good girl," I say. She gives me a little lick then pulls away and crawls back over to Cathy's lap.

Is Anyone Sleeping?

It is a dark and stormy night and I'm awake at 1:43 a.m. I step out of bed and right onto Mary's tail.

"Sorry, Mary," I say as I make my way to Eli's kennel. "Eli, up." He jumps into the kennel and I latch the door.

"Does he have to go O.U.T.?" Mike asks. Because it's in the middle of the night, we don't want the dogs to get excited about the out word. If I weren't so tired, I would laugh.

"No, but he's been in and out of our bed about six times since 10:30 and I'm not sure why." Just then, there is a distant gentle rumble of thunder. "Oh, that's why." Eli is afraid of thunder.

I crawl back between the covers and Sally darts out from under them. She sits on my arm. I try scooching her over, but she turns and licks my face. That's code for I need to go out. I get back out of bed. "Come on, let's go."

"Why don't you take Eli, too?"

"He's not going to go outside when it's thundering." I unlatch the kennel and call him. He peers at me from the dark depths of the cage, but doesn't move.

Sally and I head outside. The air is cool and clouds cover the dark sky. She meanders to the grass, watching for toads along the way. As we head back to the house, Eli meets us at the door. Sally runs past him as I coax him outside. He makes a beeline for the nearest bush, pees and dashes back inside.

Thunder rumbles and the wind is howling. Eli circles my legs as I walk. A puppy Prozac might be a good idea. While we're in the kitchen, Mary wanders out of the bedroom and into the living room. She is a little geared up during storms also, so I guide everyone into our bedroom and start to close the door. Mary has a different idea and slips out of the room.

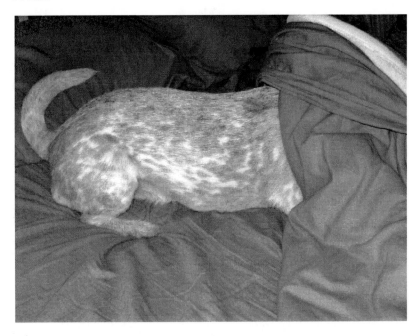

Is Anyone Sleeping?

In the dark I make my way to her pillow in the living room, careful not to jam my toes on the furniture. I reach down to pick her up and she runs off. I follow her around the couch and back to her pillow where she lets me pick her up. While I carry her to the bedroom, Eli jumps at us like an overactive jack-in-the-box. I carry Mary to her pillow in the bedroom and turn to go back and close the door. She dashes past me and tears back into the living room.

"Come on," I whine. I consider just letting her stay out there when a flash of lightning brightens the room. Using the light, I see her standing in the far hallway. Once I get her back in my arms, I close the bedroom door before I set her on the floor.

"Is Sally in the bed?" I ask Mike.

He pats the mattress. "No."

"Sally." I check the doggy pillow, her kennel and swish my feet under the clothes in the closet. No Sally.

I creep back into the living room and check the couch and doggy pillow. Still no Sally. Did I leave her outside? I open the front door and look out. No Sally. Mary takes a step toward the open door and I close it fast.

I herd Mary back into the bedroom.

"Mike, cover your eyes." I turn on the light and look under the bed. *What the heck? Where is she?* As I head back to the bedroom door Sally wanders out of the closet. "Where were you, Sal?"

It is 2:07 and Eli is back in his kennel, Mary is on her pillow and Sally is in the bed. Turning off the light, I slip between the covers and by the time my head hits the pillow,

Eli is licking my face. I didn't even hear him get out of his kennel.

"Okay Eli, okay, okay, okay, okay. Enough with the licking." I wipe the doggy spit covering my cheeks and mouth with the edge of the pillowcase. He is quick with his tongue and has a penchant for lips. I calm him down and he lies beside me. Sally has crawled under the covers and is lying in the cave, the space behind my bent knees. We lay in a lump, listening to the thunder in the distance.

"Mary, quit," Mike says. I wake with a start and it is 2:25. I have slept 18 minutes.

"What is she doing?" I ask wearily.

"Banging against the bed," he says. "Come here, Mary." He lifts her up on the bed and she lies against my legs.

Is Anyone Sleeping?

I am now a doggy sandwich. Eli is wedged against my left side, with Mary burrowed against my legs on the same side. Sally stretches along my legs, under the blankets, on my right. And of course, I have to pee.

I pull myself out of the covers and pad across the floor to the bathroom. When I return, I crawl into bed between Sally and Eli. Putting my head on the pillow, I find Mary. She is lying across my pillow, trembling. I put one hand on her, and the other on Eli. Sally wraps herself around my legs. Mike is stretched across his half of the king bed with no animal disrupting his space.

At last, we all quiet down, but I am wide awake. After several minutes, I feel Mary's trembling stop, Eli's breathing is normal and Sally has stopped licking my leg. I relax and begin to doze off.

Then Mary stands and walks across my head.

Door Paranoia

"Come on, Sal," I say. Eli looks at her then up at me. I think I detect a slight shaking of his head as if to imply she is nuts. "Yup, she's a little odd, Eli."

In Sally's world, when walking through an opening, such as a door, no part of her body should touch anything. Therefore, with the door only open a foot, Sally is unable to walk through it without her shoulders bumping the door-frame. This is not going to work for the little princess. Eli barges past her and sits by my chair. Sally skids to a stop outside and stares at the opening.

When we moved into our new house, I was apprehensive about setting up my office downstairs. I had tried a home office before, but the dogs interrupted me on an hourly basis. A cold snout was always bumping my arm or leg, vying for my attention. Plus, constant barking at the door signaled a need to go outside. I was up and down from my desk, in and out the door, and getting no work done. I was getting a lot of exercise, though.

So the first adjustment at the new house is the dogs' constant in and out. They want to be outside and I don't blame them. It is a great back yard with a pond full of fish and frogs to investigate. However, I will not be getting work done if I let them outside all the time. I solve this problem by leaving the screen door open about a foot. This works great for everyone except, you guessed it, the little white dog.

Sally moves toward the open door, sticks her head through the opening, and then backs up. I laugh out loud.

"You're kidding me, right?" She gives me the Sally evil eye.

She repeats this maneuver over and over and I am just about to get up and let her in when I decide to play with her a little. I know it sounds crazy, but I'm a little bored and Sally's idiosyncrasies never fail to entertain.

I screw the top off the treat container, which gets everyone's attention. Eli sits, Mary rouses herself from her nap in the corner, and Sally stares through the screen.

"Sit," I say and everyone does, even Sally although she is still outside. I give Eli and Mary a doggy biscuit.

"Come on, Sally," I say, holding the treat toward the door. Eli sneaks over and snatches it out of my hand quick as a frog snaps up a fly.

"No, Eli." I scold him. "That was for the nut case outside."

Sally sticks her head through the opening of the door. "Come on, Sal. You can do it." She puts one paw in, bumps her shoulder on the screen frame and double-steps backwards. This is crazy.

"Treat, Sally." I hold the snack toward her. "Come get your treat."

I do this several times until my arm gets tired from holding the biscuit toward her. I have just decided to end the game and open the door when she bursts through. Her body bangs against the screen and the doorframe, but she flies through and grabs the snack from my hand.

"Good girl," I say as I pat her head. "What a brave girl you are."

While giving her praise, a chipmunk scoots by the door outside. Eli is up and outside with Mary chasing close behind him. Sally spins around and follows Mary until she gets to the door and makes an abrupt stop. Wiggling and whining, she turns and stares at me until I open the screen wider. She bolts past me and down to the pond where she splashes into the water.

"Door, no," I shout to her. "But pond, yes?"

She turns her head and looks at me, water dripping from her mouth. She does a full body shake, and then runs to Eli who is busy sniffing every crevice along the house.

I walk back into the house, leaving the door wide open.

The Butterfly Stalker

I pull weeds from my garden and throw a clump into the driveway. It lands on Eli who is keeping a close eye on my work. As I clear weeds from a large patch of orange day lilies, Mary ambles over and settles in the middle of the plants.

"You're not very subtle, are you Mary?" I give her some loving and look around for the little white dog but don't see her. My guess is that she is down at the pond with that long snout of hers rooting in the mud.

Our house is a bi-level with a three-tier wall built into the landscape bordering the driveway. The garden is the top level, the second has rose bushes and the bottom has butterfly bushes, gladiolas and more roses.

I shade my eyes with my hand and look over the wall at the pond, searching for Sally. She is nowhere to be seen, so I walk closer to the edge and see her on the second tier. She is staring at the butterfly bush whose flowers are alive with fluttering butterflies. Sally stands still and a yellow one lands on a blossom inches from her nose. Wish I had my camera. But

I don't and by the time I run inside to get it she will be off to something else. Sally has a short attention span.

I return to weeding and after 15 minutes, I'm finished for the day. Sally is still staring at the bush so I run inside and grab my camera. When I return, she is frozen in the same position. I snap about 20 photos of her and the butterflies.

The following morning, I'm having breakfast with the editor of <u>Cats and Dogs Magazine</u> and tell her about Sally and the butterflies.

"I want to write a story about it," I say. "But something needs to happen. Right now, all she's doing is staring."

Later I'm working in my home office. My desk overlooks the back yard, and only a few feet away from the window is another butterfly bush, one of three along the three-tier wall. The bushes are again alive with butterflies. This photo opportunity cannot pass so I grab my camera and dash outside. Sally follows me.

As I take pictures of the bushes near my window, I see Sally standing on the second tier of the wall staring into another butterfly bush. She stands dead still and watches the butterflies as they light, fly away and return. Nothing on her is moving, not even her ears. Only her eyes move as she watches the butterflies come and go. Not even a muscle ripples.

Snapping photos as fast as possible, I tiptoe toward her. Sally is averse to getting her picture taken so I don't want to get too close and interrupt her obvious concentration. Or is this a new obsession? I peer at her face. Hitting the zoom lens, I keep inching forward. A foot away from the bush she turns and looks at me. I freeze. Then she turns her gaze back to the bush.

Meanwhile, Eli is chasing a butterfly across the yard, leaping into the air. Like the day before, Mary is dozing in the day lilies letting the sun warm her old body.

I wander around the yard and try to get close-ups of the flowers and different butterflies. A yellow one is elusive, and my goal is to get a good photo. I keep checking on Sally and sure enough, she is in the same place.

I'm still not sure how this will become a column since a story about her staring at butterflies for hours isn't very exciting.

I move around the bush, snapping photos from different angles. Sally is so cute peeking through the bush, intent on the butterflies. The yellow one lands only inches from her nose again and this time I have my camera. This picture is going to be unbelievable!

I click the button on my camera, Sally's long nose inches closer and she snatches that beautiful butterfly right into her mouth. What? I am aghast.

"Sally!" I step back and watch as she munches on it. The cute butterfly gazer has become the butterfly eater. A minute later, another butterfly gets too close and snatch! That is two gone. At this rate, there will be no butterflies left in the bushes.

I wave my arms and Sally gives me the evil eye.

"Oh stop," I say. "Come on, you little killer."

After coaxing her away from the bush, she trots to the pond where she laps water for several minutes. I guess eating butterflies causes dry mouth. I grab my cell phone and call my editor.

"Guess what," I say. "I have my butterfly story, but it's not pretty."

About the Author

Tricia L. McDonald is an internationally published author, public speaker and entrepreneur who lives and writes in Grand Haven, Michigan.

Her first book in this series, <u>Life With Sally: Little White Dog Tails</u>, is a compilation of stories chronicling life with her miniature bull terrier, and was published in December 2009.She also writes a monthly column, Life With Sally, for *Cats and Dogs Magazine* (www.catsanddogsmagazine.com).

Tricia's humorous and touching accounts of life have been published in *The Breastfeeding Diaries*, Meadowbrook Press, 2007; *Mom Writer's Literary Magazine*, Summer 2007; *A Cup of Comfort for Mothers & Sons*, Adams Media, 2005; and *A Cup of Comfort for Mothers*, Adams Media, February 2010.

As a writing coach, Tricia owns A Writing Passage, where she has a hands-on approach to guiding others in the writing process. Tricia helps writers prepare their manuscripts for publication, facilitates writing groups, edits manuscripts, and works one-on-one with writers to hone their writing skills. She holds a BA in English with a Creative Writing Emphasis from Grand Valley State University.

You can reach Tricia at www.awritingpassage.com or email her at triciawrite@charter.net.

Life With Sally
Little White Dog Tails

and

Life With Sally
Still Spinnin' Tails

can be purchased online at
awritingpassage.com, splatteredinkpress.com
and amazon.com

or by mail at

Splattered Ink Press
16637 Rich Street
Grand Haven, MI 49417

$13.95 + $3.99 shipping

Your copy will be autographed by Sally.